Frances Writes a Fable

Branca Tani

Rosen Classroom
New York

Frances is writing a fable.
A fable is a story
that teaches a lesson.
The lesson is called a moral.

Most fables are about animals.
Animals in fables usually
talk to each other.
They act like people.

Frances writes a fable about a family of ducks and a wolf. They are the characters in the story.

Her fable takes place
in the forest.
The forest is the setting
of the story.

Frances's fable begins
with a family of ducks
that go for a walk.
One of the babies gets lost.
This is the plot of the story.

The baby duck is lost.

He cannot find his mom.

He is alone and scared.

The baby duck asks other animals for help.
No animal will help.
It is late, and they are tired.

The baby duck sees a wolf.
He is afraid to ask
the wolf for help.
The wolf is scary.

In the end, the wolf is friendly.
The wolf helps the duck
to find his mom.
This is how Frances's fable ends.

The moral of Frances's fable is not to think badly about someone.

Words to Know

duck

family

forest

wolf